MW01110260

O

Custodians

by Robin Nelson
photographs by Stephen G. Donaldson

Lerner Publications Company • Minneapolis

Lerner Publications Company
A division of Lerner Publishing Group
241 First Avenue North
Minneapolis, MN 55401 USA

Website address: www.lernerbooks.com

Words in **bold type** are explained in a glossary on page 31.

Library of Congress Cataloging-in-Publication Data

Nelson, Robin, 1971–
    Custodians / by Robin Nelson.
        p.   cm. – (Pull ahead books)
    Includes index.
    ISBN: 0–8225–1687–X (lib. bdg. : alk. paper)
    1. School custodians–Juvenile literature. [1. School custodians. 2. Custodians.] I. Title. II. Series.
LB3235.N35 2005
371.6'8–dc22   2003023291

Manufactured in the United States of America
1 2 3 4 5 6 – JR – 10 09 08 07 06 05

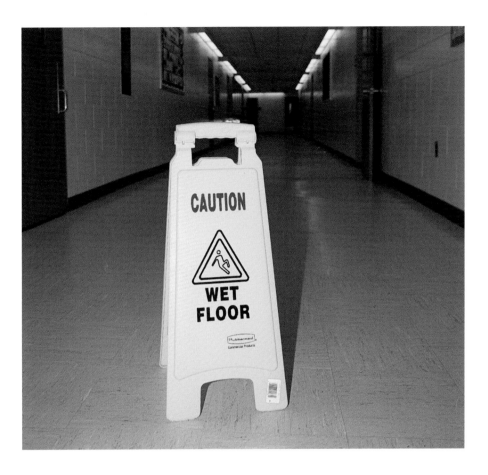

"Be careful! The floor is wet," says the voice in the hall. Whose voice is it?

It is the voice of a custodian. Custodians are people in your **community.**

Custodians take care of buildings in your community. Your school has custodians.

Custodians are important people.
They must be there when something
goes wrong in a building.

Custodians carry
pagers or phones with
them. They can be
called from far away.

Custodians carry many keys. They can unlock any door in a school.

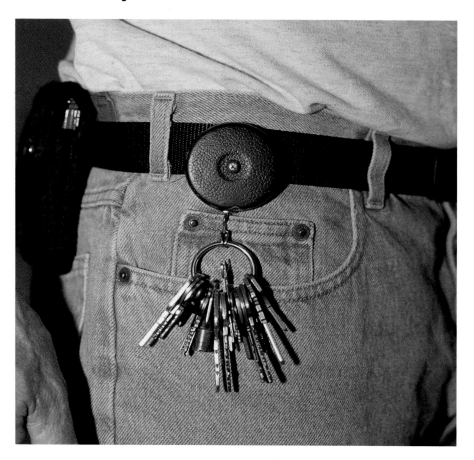

Custodians unlock a school's doors in the morning. They lock the doors at night.

Custodians can fix almost anything in a school. They use tools, such as hammers, nails, and **drills.**

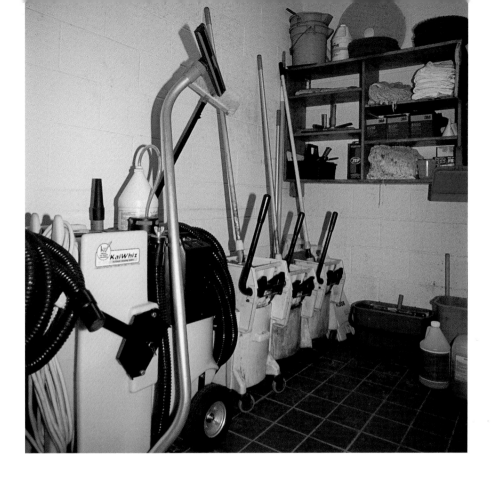

Custodians use mops, brooms, and other tools to keep a school clean. Custodians keep their tools in a big closet.

Custodians
clean carpets.

Custodians throw away garbage at the
end of each day.

Floors in **cafeterias** are messy after
lunch. Custodians mop the floors.

Sometimes custodians **polish** floors.
Custodians make the floors shine.

Custodians make a school look nice.
They plant flowers and trees.

Custodians take care of plants by
watering them.

Custodians paint the walls in classrooms.

Custodians want teachers and students to have bright and clean classrooms for the school year.

Custodians fix things that break in a school.

A lightbulb has burned out. A custodian will change the lightbulb.

21

Boilers keep schools warm. Custodians make sure boilers are working.

What if custodians can't fix something?
They call someone to help.

Custodians also keep schools safe.
They throw away things that might
hurt kids.

Custodians make sure playgrounds are safe to play on.

Custodians like students. Custodians
want students to have a clean and
safe school.

Custodians are proud of their work. Students are proud of their custodians.

Facts about Custodians

■ Many custodians work at night after most people have gone home.

■ Custodians are sometimes called janitors.

■ Many custodians live near the building where they work. They are important members of the community. You might have a custodian living in your neighborhood.

■ Some custodians wear special clothes when they are at work. These clothes are called uniforms.

■ Custodians must be good at working with other people. Custodians have to work with people, such as students, teachers, and other custodians.

Custodians through History

■ Custodians use brooms to clean buildings. The first brooms were made from a plant called broomcorn. A factory began making these brooms in the United States in 1859.

■ Many years ago, schools did not have custodians. Teachers did many of the jobs that custodians do. Teachers made sure that students had a clean place where they could learn.

■ Schools did not always have boilers to keep students and teachers warm. Schools used to have small stoves that burned wood. Students would bring some wood from home each morning for the stove.

More about Custodians

Check out these books and websites about custodians.

Books

Klingel, Cynthia Fitterer, Robert B. Noyed, and Cindy Klingel. *School Custodians.* Vero Beach, FL: Rourke Publishing, 2001.

Morris, Ann. *That's Our Custodian!* Minneapolis: Millbrook Press, 2003.

Nelson, Robin. *School Then and Now.* Minneapolis: Lerner Publications Company, 2003.

Weber, Valerie, and Gloria Jenkins. *School in Grandma's Day.* Minneapolis: Carolrhoda Books, 1999.

Websites

"Remembering the Little Red Schoolhouse." http://www.americaslibrary.gov/cgi-bin/page.cgi/es/mn/schlhse_1

"One-Room Schoolhouse." http://www.americaslibrary.gov/cgi-bin/page.cgi/es/ny/school_1

Glossary

boilers: machines that keeps buildings warm

cafeterias: rooms in a school where students eat lunch

community: a group of people who live in the same city, town, or neighborhood. Communities share the same fire departments, libraries, schools, and other helpful places.

drills: tools that make holes

pagers: machines used to call people from far away

polish: to rub and make shine

Index

Photo Acknowledgments

All photographs appear courtesy of Stephen G. Donaldson with the exception of the following image: © State Historical Society of North Dakota, p. 29.